Black Flowers

Adaptations from

Kaviyarasu Na. Kamarasan's Poetries

in english

Sanna Ratnavel

Dedicate this book to the thousands of dusty soil footpaths which accommodate poor comrades for their sleep during the night – **Na.Kamarasan,**   **1.04.1971**.

Contents

*****

Foreword

Translating or adaptation from a classical language to English poses significant challenges. It's not about lacking superior vocabularies in either language, but rather about capturing the nuances and intentions of the original poet's expression.

Understanding the poet's message and selecting the appropriate words to convey it accurately is no easy achievement.

The translator must ideally share the same cultural background and sensibilities as the poet to truly grip the essence of the work and effectively convey it in another language.

My husband, Kaviyarasu Na.Kamarasan, a remarkable poet of the past six decades, stands out similar to ancient luminaries such as Wordsworth, Tagore, and Bharathi.

He gained widespread popularity and acclaim, not only for his poetry but also for his contributions as a lyricist in Tamil cinema (Tollywood). His songs were deemed extraordinary by seasoned poets and resonated deeply with audiences, including prominent figures in the state.

My younger brother, Dr.Sanna Ratnavel had the unique advantage of being raised in the same cultural environment as the esteemed poet, thanks to his mother's role as the poet's school teacher.

Sharing a similar poetic sensibility, he undertook the immense task of translating Kaviyarasu.Kamarasan's works into English. Despite his busy schedule, he dedicated himself to this endeavour, and the result is a book that has been scrutinized and praised by the poet's close associates and literary scholars.

The translated poems are said to closely mirror the original content and essence, a witness to my Brother Dr.Sanna Ratnavel's skill and dedication.

I am deeply grateful to my brother, Dr.Sanna Ratnavel for fulfilling the request of my husband, the poet, Kaviyarasu.Kamarasan to bring his works from the land of classic Tamil literature to the wider audience of English literature. I extend my heartfelt wishes for his success in all his future endeavours.

I hope readers will find joy in exploring the English renditions and exploring into the cultural connections they offer.

My best wishes go out to all readers as they pursue their ambitions with enthusiasm and determination.

Yours Faithfully

Logamani Kamarasan

(W/O Kaviyarasu Na.Kamarasan)

15.04.2024

Preface

Poetry is tears but for me it is the mother's milk as assume myself as a child. As a small child when you sleep in frustration cradle quietly, poets are attacked by tragedies. It is not a surprise to me. Poetry is meant not for the country, language, race etc., but should travel beyond these boundaries like a bird spread its wings beyond the world boundaries. I leave it to you and weigh these poems with your wisdom. I am grateful to **'Kavignar .Kannadasan'** for his prologue.

Sincerely

Na.Kamarasan,   **01.04.1971**

****

In school, I received this original book from a friend and questioned its title, believing I knew everything. I was affluent but rejected ideologies, except those of the 'Red movement'. The book used "Black Color" and "Fetus or Nucleus" interchangeably, perplexing me. I inferred "black in color or nucleus," both addressing less privileged issues.

As the book was poetic, I analyzed each poem, its transformations, and conclusions. Now, it's popular among intellectuals. The poet, coincidentally from my native village where my mother taught the poet, his wife and children too, as a primary school teacher, asked me to translate it.

Five decades later, with gained confidence, I translated it. Born from the same soil, I felt connected to the poet's thoughts and feelings. This honor, despite my prestigious education, immersed me in the poet's world.

Thanking you

Sanna Ratnavel,   **15.04.2024.**

Acknowledgments

I extend my heartfelt gratitude to the poet's family, close associates, and esteemed friends for entrusting me with the translations. Their acceptance and encouragement fueled my dedication, often leading to sleepless nights immersed in the original content and the poet's expressive techniques. It's remarkable how a writer's work can captivate to the point of foregoing sleep.

 I am deeply thankful to the publishers for their unwavering support in bringing this content to fruition in book format.

 I urge readers to ponder upon the text, recognizing it as the voice of the marginalized worldwide. While I may not have all the answers, I invite readers to engage critically and discover their own ideologies within these pages.

Sanna Ratanvel

PROLOGUE

Kavignar Kannadasan

When the mind is comfortable, the spirit, imagination, and desires join as a catalyst, and delicious poems are delivered.

The poems are construed as rare pearls when unlimited thoughts flow unrestricted. Naturally, there shall be feelings of spiritual justice in the minds of a poet, who usually creates highly reasonable poems in his writings.

In the fingers of an eminent artist, if the brush dances celebrating colors, bring the best painting, sometimes more than expected in the result.

 If you synthesize the words and meanings in the form of a sensible craft, the poem also expresses its delightful messages to society. When the poet's emotions are not strong, he always thinks of less privileged people. Then, agreeing, neglecting, and repositioning his stand are consequences of emotions.

When the poet repositions and gives consent different from the previous land-up with conflicts, reasonable society must come forward to acknowledge the reason for the conflict. The poet's soul is like a flood. It is exposed as a surge in any spot he prefers.

Anyone who raises a question in the poems written by the poet, to be answered by the person who raised the question. Answering a question raised by readers is not the job of a poet.

Whatever the poet says, all are his justifications. He can't feed the acceptable contents for dissimilar populations.

A poet invites the hungry mass to lunch, which he prefers to host. The leaf he spreads for food is his own decision.

 The hungry men with good stomachs take food from the food court. The poet is unable to identify the real hungry people.

Only hungry masses sit in the food court. Hence, the poet prefers the menu and spot on his own for his satisfaction only.

Therefore, he submits his feast of this book 'The black Flowers' to those hungry for like-minded intellectuals. The poems remind with contents of various patterns and styles. It is possible to observe echoes of different cultures across the book.

The title of the book is new to the literature world. The theme of the poems is also innovative. The verses mesmerize with metaphors. There are many modern worlds sparkling in the flow of writings.

It is named black flowers but in white poetry.

This work is the first successful book 'The Black Flowers' in modern writing, an example of world literature. My friend Na.Kamarasan will be the most successful eminent poet of the world.

This work of the poet could be translated into English and other languages. Translation will also bring success.

With Love

KANNADASAN,

Chennai.   **Date: 27.03.1971**

1. Foot Prints

During vibrant rainbow days,

Within the kingdom of your dreams,

At the edge of the crescent of the moon,

Your poetry's policy is noticeable,

And it seems to spill in the madness,

Here, my tears are rolling down!

It is visible,

Even in the direction of sunset!

And in the fashionable shadows of spring,

Even within the morning's light,

Your imagination becomes evident!

Your envoy reaches out with a message

In each flower of the oasis!

On the inconsolable nights,

During the cuckoo's concert session,

In the weeping of the harp,

Thus, offer ablation of your tongue!

At the entry of the day,

You embed the imprint of your wisdom!

In the discourse of time,

The gloomy sound of bird wings,

On the waves of the blue sea,

In the mother tongue of rain spray,

Deep poetic voices of echoes,

Harness you to rise to the throne,

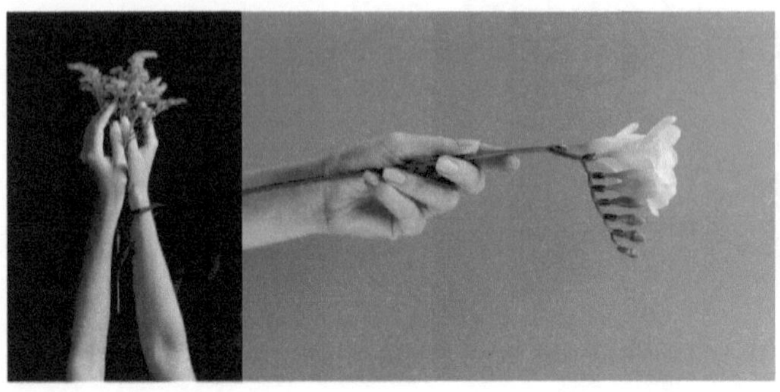

In the dryness of the flower's buds,

The daylights conceal them on the horizon,

During the seasons of leaping,

I observed the shades of your end,

On the foamy banks of the River Kaveri,

I witnessed your tears!

*****

2. A Bath of Wisdom

In the terrestrial of the Himalayan

Landscapes of picturesque dreams,

I exist as a casually spilt honey droplet,

I am the melody of the mind;

And the singer laments

All composed upon the philosophical stage!

I am a tiny foamy offspring,

Destined to traverse

The Surges of the vast ocean!

I represent the universal mantra,

As brushed by the saint's artistic hand!

I am the epic flora,

The guiding root of the truth,

Within the imagination land bed!

I am the life of the golden flag,

A cherished treasure,

And I ripened through the infancy of fruit-bearing!

I stand conquering in the wars,

Reducing the illusory mental

Fortresses to fragments!

I also dismantled the desires for the five senses,

Immersed myself in the river of wisdom

*****

3. Bougainvilleae Flowers

In the spray of the monsoon's phase,

We emerge as barren growths,

And within the life narrative

Of maternal nurturing,

We endure puzzles like riddles!

Transforming into seeds' thorns,

We turn into the blackish of a lamp's glow,

Inert muscles we have grown, Ending life as comics!

A dumb individual composes a melody,

While a disabled person scribes the verses,

Does it hold logic for a fully blind man

To peruse text carved by the physically challenged?

We become akin To the sound of the mute's song,

The text is written by the disabled

The sightless read the same,

We indicate the interstitial errors

In between the words,

Like the errors within our heredity, too!

God rectify the rulebook of creation!

As we desire, adorning flowers in our braids,

It so happens,

Arranging flowers

within a cemetery is permissible;

-Indeed,

We are a vibrant blossom cemetery!

Absolutely!

The motherly woman personifies

an Arabian Jasmine,

The solitary bare woman

Becomes a Screw Pine Flower,

We are similar to the drapery of the mouthpiece,

Labelled, born out of thorny stems,

Bougainvillea glabra- *The 'Paper flowers'*

*****

4. Moon Light Dinner

(Moon Light Dinner – The Tearful Contemplations of a Beggar on the Eve of the New Moon.Within a maternal embrace of the surface of soil earth)

I rest, a spreadsheet,

Within a golden dust's expanse,

I move forward as a youthful son

of this golden spread,

Earthquakes become my kisses

in monsoon season!

The cyclone, my lullaby,

Water transforms into

My mother's nourishing milk,

Tears wear my smile!

Hunger turns into my athletic pursuit,

Seasons mark my attire's alterations,

The burial ground serves

As my shelter of mud,

The culmination of life resembles

My profound slumber,

I remain awake,

Embracing the end of my journey!

The 'tumba' flower fractures

the moonlit night,

In this spectacle,

The celestial fish never rest!

The impending new moon

arrives tomorrow,

The day is named the burial day

of the greyish moon,

I prepare to sleep within

The pale moon's dominion;

The crescent moon is akin

to a fragment of my meal,

The sky stars

 are my side dish,

Assuming this aggravates

the pang of hunger!

I await the chariot of

the God, Pluto

****

5. The Homage

Oh! My darling, beautiful woman!

Oh, my cherished lady!

On the wintery night of the ripened moon,

During the full celebration

Of Lord Krishna's festivity,

Within the depths of my heart

And the melody of my dreams,

I quest for your presence!

These quests embody my sombre message,

This pursuit is my tribute!

Within the weeping of the poetic island,

In the breath of forest blossoms

In the sorrowful dots of stars,

Within the lengthy shadows of the night,

I continue to seek you!

These searches are my gloomy message,

These searches remain my homage!

In the prolonged opus of humanity,

Within the profound sleep of inner voices,

In the songs of the universe juncture,

I relentlessly search for you!

These searches are my gloomy message,

These searches remain my homage!

*****

6. The Black Queen

Karuththamma (The poet inspired by

In the film "SEMEEN," Karuththamma is a girl

who experienced

a failed marriage and lost love.

Eventually, she and her lover end their lives

together in the sea, when they met later,

after many years)

Once upon a time,

In the igniting of poetic flame,

I beheld, just once,

You, the tonic of world literature!

You ornamented the opus of

My shattered heart,

You put on the apparel of my myths,

Yet, love swiftly reveals itself on the soils

Within the gap of time,

you occupied my associations,

Fading away like a transient dream!

Oh, ebony mother

ebony mother!

You are the CRIMSON FISH

Submerged in the depth,

You march as a procession of poetry,

Bearing verses within

The curves of your being!

You represent tearful celebrations!

Your origin proclaims

The potter named 'Lamp's Bowl' as the architect,

Oh, Daughter of Renown!

Oh, Gilded Blossom!

The earth's daydream of daughter's threshold!

Your laughter waves through the flame,

In the lanes of time,

Your daydream pilots the chariot of flowers,

Your crying continues within

The tides of the airy river!

The faded blossom of your love

Shall resurge and flourish in paradise!

May the flower that

graced the dream unfold!

On the hull of the fishing vessel,

The spread of tender sand gulps

the moon's glow akin to white wine,

And intones the hymns of its essence,

There, the LOVER sings!

May your love's bloom

Bathe amid the 'eastern rain'!

May the melodies of your soul

Awake in the prolonged tune of the FLUTE.

*****

7. The VOW

I here,

declare this VOW,

Acknowledging my conclusion,

 On behalf of the socialist flower

And the earth;

I pronounce it!

At the speed of lightning in the cloud threads,

The wind composes the rain's melody,

I penetrate through with tearful musical notes,

I pour forth the flames of revolution onto the soil!

The desert represents

the utmost dryness of the earth,

I shall transform it into a blossoming pearl sea,

I shall sharpen the cyclone

And convert them into

Numerous new southwestern breezes!

I compensate the beggars with coins

As if they were stylish,

Engaging in interactions,

Routing the sun's energy into solar heat,

Assisting the underprivileged to cook their food!

Within the gaze of the radiant lamp,

I burn the ambitions of parasites;

 In the dialects of glow,

I shall articulate the insignificance!

Within the bosom of the global grove,

I shall sing a sonnet to the ascending tree;

I shall seek justice for disorders

In the form of drops from the river Ganga,

Symbolizing blood!

*****

8. The Orphans

The Orphans! Oh, orphans,

Your poet recites,

Lightened by the radiance

of the crescent star,

Countless foamy blossoms

adorn the riverbank,

He sings in a vaporous tongue

with a silent resonance!

Oh, orphans,

Your beloved vocalist sings there!

Oh, wavering flames of lamps,

You embrace fascination!

Oh, the repose upon your spires!

You represent the melodies

of the voiceless singer,

The supports of life's absences!

You personify the relationship of earthly dust,

He sings in the evanescent tongue

with a voiceless echo!

Oh, orphan, your minstrel is singing there!

Upon the verge of poetic lines,

The offspring of dreams warble there,

A youthful mother's bosom awaits,

Wherein the wind takes the form of mother's milk!

A fertile and substantial lap is present,

The thatched roof of palm leaves carries water there,

The cure found in the singer's tears,

Brightened by the crescent star's light,

Countless bubbly blossoms grace the riverbank,

He sings in the evanescent tongue

With a voiceless echo!

Oh, orphan, your minstrel is singing there!

*****

9. The Painful Songs
Of a Tribal Group Living in Hills

The spray of summer rain,

The melodies of the Cool River,

Zenger's (Alanji) pleasure garden,

Within the confines of that forest,

The shadow of greed lies beneath the teak tree,

A honey bee's nest resides there,

We are the burglars of the palace

of the honey bee's nest!

The fake milkweed plant fountains milk

and turns barren green,

Honey sprinkles like motherhood,

Known as the sugar flower

of the southern region,

Bees alight upon the sugar-coated flower,

Creating an ecstatic hum!

Bees carry the honey,

Tree branches bear the honeyed nests,

The branches adorned with honeyed nests

Grace the hills of the south,

The peaks of the southern hills

Shall be the streets of our abode,

Milk begets curd,

The taste of honey intensifies

With every season of blooming,

Hence, we are the kind of honey gatherers!

A fledgling parrot in the cradle,

Upon the shoulder rests my peacock wife,

A wife embracing the shoulder experiences

Numerous hardships,

The moon blesses the empyrean,

Yet our stomachs remain hungry!

In our stride, a dedicated pace,

The shadow of Lord Buddha in our sleep,

In our modest huts,

a non-materialistic essence,

The entire clan teeters

on the brink of disillusionment!

We resemble forest herbs,

Concealed from the gaze of the civilized,

Living like inert bodies!

*****

10. The Blood Flowers

In the empyreans fish thorn fence,

Along the night's cloudy street,

Within the dreams festooned with eye pearls,

A scene comes into view!

A honey bee's singer,

During a sacred springtime,

A parcel of earth's terrain,

We blossomed into tangible dreams!

Within the pressure of sweat,

In the melody of the horizon water,

In the tears of eyes resembling fish,

Comrades turn into a security fund!

The fire chuckles akin to the

Elongation of nature's tongue,

Darkness dissipates akin to the laugh of the skyline

Everywhere, the splendour of blood flowers prevails!

As greenness approaches,

Within the shelter of leafy shadows,

A rose plant stands

As an embodiment of lofty aspirations!

In the autumn season,

One fine evening in the rains embrace,

The skillfulness of roses was

Fragmented by a minor turmoil!

A honey bee's songster,

During a sacred springtime,

A parcel of earth's terrain,

We blossomed into tangible dreams!

Within the honeyed nest of the 'Nimtree',

In your lush forest of gentle melodies,

Each nap's drop transforms into teardrops!

In our land,

Your song rides the winds!

We plead with you to pour the waters of your melodies

To safeguard our clans!

Lest your mythical honeyed dwelling

Transform into a graveyard,

And our eyes shall hunger for tears!

****

11. The Red Soil

During the poetic melodies' vibrations

 in the red soil earth,

Along the path of roses-laden

With the thorns of frustrations,

In the path of roses,

The figures of shyness emerge!

Sleep symbol in the tones of reddish eyes,

The silent soil ages through dreams,

Red manifests in the form

of deep meditation!

In the poetic melodies' vibrations in the red soil earth,

Along the path of roses

Filled with the thorns of frustrations!

The silken maturities transform into coral graveyards,

Melting in the rain like mythical wax!

The chariot of roses could not drawn

Along the strong wind's tether!

The soil is mixed sed with blood and life!

During the poetic melodies' vibrations

In the red soil earth,

Along the path of rose-frustration thorns!

*****

12. They Launch Enquiry On The Court!

I sprouted as a Tamil language admirer

And raised as a Socialist.

Using a humble quill,

I introduced the essence

Of spring to the working class.

I firmly believe that when my pen trembles,

it shapes a realm of governance

With resounding pride.

While I absorb ambitious dreams,

My commitment to sincere creations

My writing persists until my last breath.

Facing occasionally intolerant court behaviours,

I stand prepared to express

My perspectives through the written word.

My silence here becomes a poem of muteness.

With the aid of solitude,

This silence might metamorphose

Into vibrant scriptures,

Eventually, adapting a reasonable poetic form.

Observing the towering court buildings,

Comprehending the plight of beggars

On the streets and the earnest desires

Elderly prisoners encountered

in real life becomes a challenge.

My intense tears witness

Their longing for a dignified life,

Often thwarted by societal stigmas.

Similarly, just as the traditional schools

Of a great nation was dismantled

And revolutionary blooms suppressed,

A legal system established

To nurture socialist flowers.

The decisions of policy-oriented

Politics manipulated;

When the courts rejected it,

My boiling anger elevated the stance of the judiciary.

My poetic fury continues to resonate

Within the chambers of justice.

*****

13. The Beginning of Woman

The beggar woman

During the night-time hours,

Even in napping,

The courtroom holds a distinct respect.

Presently, we do not prostrate ourselves

before the court,

Just as we observe the footsteps

of time advancing.

As they move forward,

We cast our gaze upon prison bars

and persist forward.

What does the world hold for us?

Beyond liberating caged birds,

The commencement of your

The investigation marks the moment,

And the verdict,

The culmination behind prison walls,

Displays no compassion

I held you as the dwelling of justice,

O Just Deity, yet to the God of Justice;

You are no more than a mere balance.

Even if an address is acquired,

 It does not sway the scales of victory.

With your consent,

Justice shall encounter the Divine.

Behold, I am but a simple poet!

My vessel of justice,

Brimming with righteousness,

Steers your narrow path

In the early days of spring,

did you shape my destiny

While I etched a solitary smile,

a unique stride?

That very stride now persists

as a captive bird,

Still chirping.

Yet I, even in the night,

Stand accused in the open field.

Today, we do not plead guilty.

What does this world extend to us?

Except for the release of caged birds

*****

14. Alcohol Consumers

Oh, precious wine!

You are a regal elixir,

The nurturing milk of illustrious poets!

If you are the gilded wings of a celestial messenger,

Then to whom does this shackle belong?

If your essence is a quiet melody,

Who is this outcry from?

If you befriend pleasant dreams,

Who is this sleepless night?

Should an expert sculptor indulge in you?

Countless marvels like

The 'Taj Mahal' could have come to life;

Should painters of eminence consume you?

Numerous 'Ravi Varmas' might emerge.

And if a working-class individual

Imbibes your spirits,

Many wine glasses raised

In this world,

Even the River Nile may run dry,

Yet wine flows unrestricted.

While artistic Taj Mahals

The rarest on the earth,

And 'Ravi Varma' may not abound,

We readily permit the emptying

Of jars filled with spirits.

Oh, edifices of Justice and Tribunals,

You punish the actions of crimes

And spare the culprits.

As prison doors swing open,

The Soul of Justice draws

its windows closed.

You aren't seeds of creation;

There are no handcuffs crafted

Exclusively for courts of justice!

Justice stands with folded hands before you,

Dear courts!

Why shackle the hands of transgressions

And bear the burdens of sins on your shoulders?

Oh God of time,

Bestow the spring season upon quills

And let your gaze grace deserts

traversed by camels!

Oh! God of justice!

Scatter flowers scant on the path of camels.

On the outskirts of the courts,

Suicide prevention measures implemented,

But inside,

'Life sentence' is embraced fondly!

Why toss the arrack bottles towards villages?

This action dams

The perennial rivers

And impedes

Their aspirational dreams.

Have you ever realized?

That this is a tear shed by 'Cleopatra'?

She doesn't just bestow kisses

upon Caesar or Antony;

Her embraces extended

to all Roman soldiers.

Let us establish the city

Where 'Prohibition not imposed'

As the capital of continents,

And apply 'Prohibition' solely

to desert lands!

If feasible,

let's position the statue

of 'Mahatma Gandhi'.

We shall gaze upon coats

alongside camels

And sow 'Manila' seeds

in the shadows of date palm trees.

Arrack isn't an otherworldly elixir,

Nor is it poison.

But introduce poison into it,

And what is it then?

Is it the velocity of celestial bodies?

Or awakening post-death?

Or the cradle of dream-like

Eyelashes during slumber?

Or a skilful man

who constructs a courtyard atop a grave?

Is it brisk awareness?

Or the weight of languor on wings' chariots?

Or nectar from coconut trees?

Or the sputter of crimes?

Perhaps a procession of hair-legged soldiers?

Or a rabid Cupid's hound?

Is it silence or chatter?

Or solitary debates?

Is it peaceful slumber?

Or swimming wakefulness?

Or a drool?

Or a manifestation of blood?

Or horseback riding within the tubes of the digestive tract?

Or clutching a lust umbrella beneath

The unconscious guilt of an angelic mind?

Is it a honey jar born from a fire flower?

Or a hunger within hunger?

Or a single dream of the mind's

Calculation manifesting as two?

Or the sensation of signatures?

Whatever "it may be," it grants permits to lofty residents

While shackling the less privileged,

in arrack consumption!

Prayers still reside in slums,

Aligned with Gandhian ideals,

But sleep luxuriates in opulent domains.

Once we position the Gandhi statue,

No

Harm in repeating such actions

If they are beneficial,

Even breaking the goat milk pot and peeling peanut skins!

Once again, let us induct the statue of Gandhi!

No Wrongdoing,

in doing what's good once more.

And remember,

the permit for drinking granted

To palace dwellers,

While handcuffs adorn the impoverished consuming
arracks!

Oh, dear Courts!

If you are ascending,

Who possesses the sunsets?

If you embody the melody of justice,

Who owns the cries and tears?

Oh, dear Courts,

If you are the divine God of Justice

Who then possesses these handcuffs?

*****

15. The Grass

Sprouting from the earth's tail,

The fertile sign of spring,

The body,

A slender plant,

I label thee the chamber of snowdrop's end.

Thriving and thoroughly drenched

Dancing blades,

reaped each day,

The sustenance of smooth feet,

A rhyme to the shade of green,

The nourishing storehouse

Of Lord Krishna's friend **"Kuselar[1]"**;

Without leaping and falling

For the embrace of seawater,

Acquired a savour of salt,

An artistic, the grass!

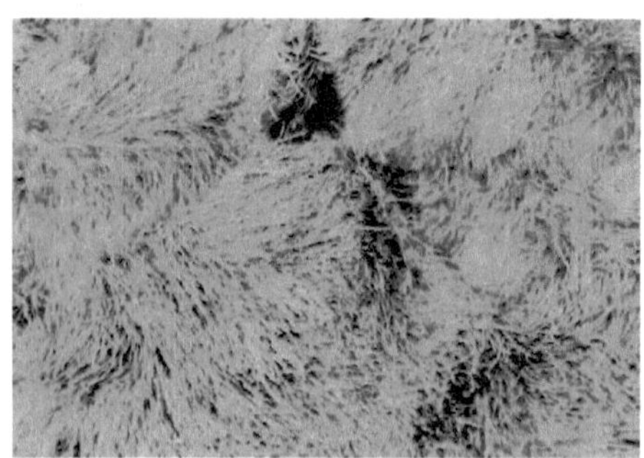

*****

16. The Foot Path

The monsoon,

A land of disorder,

An evening's paradise,

In the summer season

The classic choreographer,

A cascade of moonlight,

A meandering brook;

An ownerless expanse, neglected;

Needy rest induced by nature,

A bed of dust was created!

*****

17. The Tender Leaf

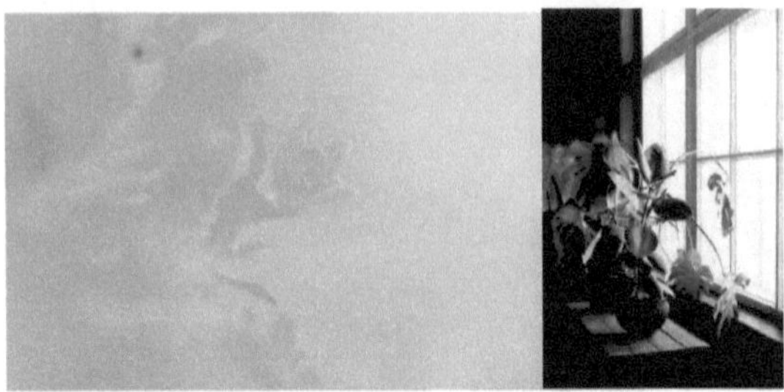

Sprouted, Leafhopper,

Kind of,

Botanical illumination,

Verbal brushstroke art;

Spring charge,

Sunshine,

The genuine darling of the household:

The deceptive offshoot of the stem,

Nature's dream,

The dry leaf sprout,

Sprout's dry leaf!

*****

18. The Dust

oh! Spared earth,

It shall bear you above,

The hurricane has arrived,

With dry leaf Saint,

Maintaining connection,

The myth of rubbish is nurtured

Hear this, you unfortunate soul!

You in the afternoon,

Sidewalk fireworks!

Even in the month,

In the wind season strikes the eyes,

A tool of the wind?

For The flower hands of cultural women,

The laziness of the soil tempts the morning labour!

Rain-soaked mud, Is it your reincarnation?

A poor farmer's garment,

O wanderer's land!

On the whole, the earth is a shared banner,

As it soars, even your dust!

*****

19. Bulbul Birds and Rose Garden

Rose gardens and 'Bulbul' birds,

Bathed in the lone crescent light,

Brightened by the

The entire stream's glow,

Like beats of a forehead's pulse,

The rose garden sheds tears,

Forestalling the snowy night,

Within dreams of spring,

Little blades of grass

Creeks not in sight!

Evening's ghostly embrace,

Tears from the Rennet tree,

On the bosom of the bushes,

The wind's cries in silence,

On periodic screens,

In the shadows of time,

Artful small garden,

Plenteous with elements!

Toddy is like a false light in the ambit,

Crescent in a dishonest boat,

The heart drifts along,

The blackish shadow's image flourishes!

Shining fish,

Swimming in the light and dark,

Feeding makes them fatter,

The sky glares,

Begging dreams,

Tears in the house of eye,

Honeycomb and the rose garden also slice,

And beneath the shadow of the skyline,

Sprouts of soil come into view!

Colors are in a feature,

Life as a division,

Without review,

That splits the eye!

The summer arriving,

It vanishes unsuccessfully,

Restoration in the Skyline melody

Bring the rainy day to a close!

Gatherings,

Seasons of falling leaves,

The traditional poet's

'Bul Bul' music,

Remains intangible!

In the lone crescent light,

In the glory of the time-old stream,

Like pulses of a forehead's beat,

The rose garden is shedding tears!

*****

20. The Postman and a Disenfranchised Village

The winter month

Shall shape a crescent moon,

I wish to say goodnight,

After the sun dissolves

The bouncy rain clouds,

I desire it speaks!

The porter of inscriptions,

Our hometown's postman,

In the invisible dusk evening,

What has fallen on us?

In-ground, decaying mud,

A royal man came for

Polishing the floor,

Why has he gone beneath the surface?

Why does he prefer solitary rest?

Long-durable henna,

Shadow-writing pen,

Behind the fall of the pen,

White inscriptions are everywhere!

Gathering the scarce money,

Owning golden rupees,

We shopped during the full moon,

But the full rupees are not honoured!

Sheets upon leaf sheets,

Bring bundles upon bundles,

The roof does not stand firm,

The rain spray leaks through!

At the distance village court,

Even as the light shines,

The light in the eye doesn't bulb,

The fiction of Vyasa has not yet ended!

Having given a post letter,

What is amiss?

The lord of Yama seems unaccountable!

Baking fire is the colour of the post box,

Here all the people are posting letters,

There is the birth and death of the postman!

*****

21. The Dumb

I am a silent march,

A cemetery for the tongue,

Sleep sprouting in legs and arms,

A tearful lake for the poet,

A beautiful painting,

I am a charming witch,

By the melody of plants,

By the sprout of words,

Yet to be discovered,

A barren land of flesh!

I don't bite the word fruits by mouth,

I am a disciple of beauty,

I am the vehicle in one way path

In bearing the words' meaning

The nest of eyes and eyebrows

Joins with a strong suit at the junction

And makes me write plenty of tearful poems,

Blind... the day's sleep of creation,

I am, it's a daydream!

I am a silent march,

A cemetery for the tongue!

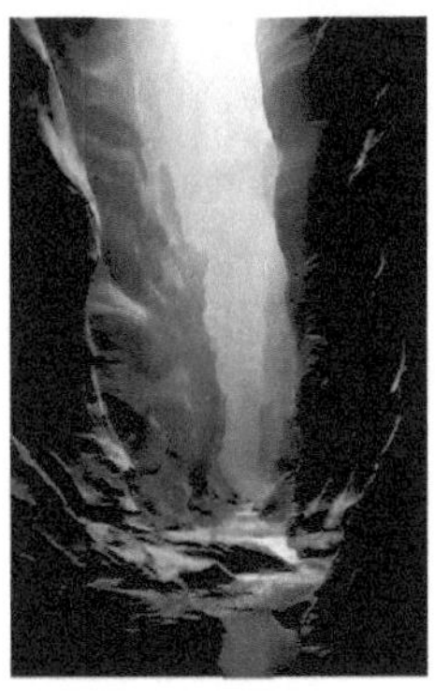

*****

22. The Clouds of the Day

In the celestial reservation,

Dawn's silver lamp shines,

For those with incapacities,

The stream of light gleams!

In spring,

He reads the word,

Bitterness turns into sweetness,

Seasons are approaching!

God blessed me

In the minds of celestial eyes,

As spiritual dreams,

He creates a multitude!

In the cradle of the tongue,

Children of weeping words,

A clan of flowers,

Transform silence into a treasure!

In the wind of isolated habitat,

He leads the prayer,

On getting on the Chariot of the Sun,

He ignites the fire of charity!

Within thatched huts,

He chuckles in the glow,

Screams in the sweat's drops of the poor,

Crying in each drop!

The Roots of Lightning,

The blossoms of rain pearls,

Fascinates the soil,

The day transforms into clouds.

*****

23. The Rainbow

This vindictive skyline,

Poured with raindrops,

And also drying the clothes,

This turns a garland woven

without fibres!

Whenever it is touched,

Rain's fibres intertwine;

And the skyline throws away

The rain upon the earth!

This eyebrow holds such beauty,

On this account, the eyes turn blind,

This flower bridge

was built on spring

Could climb up over up again!

Within the rain and the hot sun,

There is a double attack,

For whom is this mask intended?

What constitutes a parrot to drop its wings?

Who is the hunter?

Who crafted the nets of nets?

To hunt the souls of humans in the skyline?

 Is it a storied palace of colours

Or

A lonely path of beauty?

Is it a set-out greeting porch circle?

For the sky birds?

Nature, Ponder upon creating a brush,

But it constructed a painting,

Oh! See the rainbow!

Even a piece of straw,

Expelled from heaven

It is fabulous!

*****

24. The Ocean

Before this time,

At some point,

Many ages ago,

I was born right here!

The earth exists

Before I was born,

Though my hair is grey

And white as the sand,

I am still blessed

With a long blue braid!

With my long blue hair,

I wear it as something

For a while, thrown away,

They are simple dried flowers,

You mention the 'sun and the moon'!

All I get is pimples,

They dissolve into the air,

I do spend bubble foam,

And saving the pearls!

For heaven and earth,

When I weave the rain,

There are the broken threads of lightning,

I believe

And I am crying in that memory!

I am a trench of pearls,

The spread land of the ship,

The tomb of the rivers!

I bark frequently,

The reason is,

I am the hunting hound

Of the Tornado!

*****

25. The Eyes

The eyes are this universe,

Dayflowers of the forest,

Treasure of the eyelids,

Of the petal yawning dance,

Choreographer!

Next to the eyebrow flag,

Inside the gold eye lace,

Forming and tilled,

Stamps of the soul!

In the flower of the soul,

Infused with honey,

Salty spit,

Dumb beetles,

First time on soil,

As the man walks,

The path was showing,

The lights of the bridge!

In Mother's Worm Park,

In the Royal spring season,

Those that blossomed into a tent,

A day of silence and dreams!

To see the daylight,

The creator has bestowed it,

It resembles the woman's lamps

Usually, service to god,

Blindfolded artistic statue

With makeup!

Imaginative Vision Peaks,

Tears of Brahmas,

A drop in the eyelids,

Classic dance in music,

Silent dances,

Of mind region messengers,

A mental bird in search of prey,

After a little while, he opened the two mouths,

The twin flames of the headlamp,

A lamp extinguished

As it forgets to breathe

*****

26. The Larks

Two per person

Begging bowls,

You are asking me,

I walk on foot,

I run with wings,

On my wings,

Music is enchanting!

I gazed at the stars,

I eat worms!

I, from earth to heaven,

The first pilgrim,

The expansive Skylimit

The master of swimming,

Child of the Earth,

The force of attraction on a gravity rope,

It was when I sang in the skyline for the first time,

Above that is heaven,

You have started speaking!

To capture me

The king of clouds' eyes is

Like a woven mesh,

A rainbow, I sing love!

I construct a nest with broken wings.

*****

27. He is resting in peace

Sparkles in the chilling night air,

Near the snow-covered pasture,

Foam blooms on a waving flag,

Like the dreams of an artist's life,

Included in the waste of flower blooms,

In his time of need,

Right by the beach,

He is sleeping!

In the light pouring like rain,

on a full moon day,

His thoughts are like fire,

To save the people,

After meeting at the crossroads,

Right next to the beach,

He's sleeping!

In the hot sun mid-day

Also led a procession,

Envision the small hope shadows of

The freedom flag!

By looking at it,

He forgot his hunger!

Like a dance queen wearing

Foot leg anklet armament,

He enjoyed his handcuffing

Loved the event of that day!

Sparkles in the chilling night air,

While near the pasture,

Where white snow wept,

There! That beach belongs to you,

And resting in peace!

*****

28. Springs! Those old days

Those old days open

As heartfelt feelings as spring!

That blooms there in the desert

The dark shadow at that pole

That never dawns and laughs!

Vietnam's river

Of blood is shining.

Those old days open

As heartfelt feelings are springtime

That blooms there in the desert.

One day at the Bullet Wood shrine,

Thousands of thousands

Of flowers bloom in the soil.

Seek the springs of the soul,

Punishments! Dear comrades!

That spring has come now

The flower of my tears spilling!

Those old days

displayed a heartfelt feeling as spring.

That blooms there in the desert.

The historical expansive

Sea of tears,

This rose in the war

Of the life paddle of boats,

That sings the ragas of the soul.

You slept in the wave's lap grave!

The same beach,

As the eye flower is shedding tears.

Those old days open

As heartfelt feelings as spring.

That blooms there in the desert.

The flag of the age that

Turns all directions to the east.

A troop of youth walks

Through the shadows.

Seek the springs of the soul.

All youth, let's get into action.

Young comrades in the same spring soil.

We cry lullaby ourselves to sleep.

Those old days open

As heartfelt feelings as spring,

That blooms there in the desert!

*****

29. We Live Under the Sky

(The poet spent many silent nights. He wanted to write an anthem for the world's unity and suffered in his dreams. One fine morning, the eminent poet's pen moved as the blood turned into a flood of spirit and started writing the anthem of the world. Oh, my dear world, please listen to my story)

He treads on a snowdrop at dawn

He comes with a dream of liberation!

The river of deadly racism

The one who drank it gathered like an ocean!

Growing sleep in road dust

And saw his face in the moonbeam

Glistening in the morning sun

He is coming to see the future!

Russians Chinese English

My motherland lives in my blood

Muslims, American and developed nations

Vietnam witnesses blood sealing through eyeballs!

He comes with a breezy walk

And destroyed the walls of our nation

The claim of the world should be in one voice

The work concluded as true and real!

(The rationalist people forget the inequality

And meeting the eminent poet who writes

the history of the world in springtime?)
(People Meets the Great Poet)

People:

Oh, he is the son of a great poet.

The inner mind raises the divine fire

For the welfare of the earth!

The Great Poet:

Oh! Ocean of humanity!

I'm on the horizon of speaking to you

How did you become like this?

From where you are coming?

People:

Our country does not hold jails

We broke the handcuff of the boundaries

And mergerged with all

We are meeting on this day

And today is a historic day!

In the autumnal blackish crescent moon

On the soil of this poor earth

Murder frenzy wars!

A lot of Human bodies lying down on a hill

And the blood turns into reddish rivers!

The day and night turn into untruth

The tender children's heads are going away

In the smell of mother's milk

Accumulated weapon destroyed

We all gathered in love to fight!

That's when gathered with one

A sleeping human being in a chest nest

Enjoyed singing!

In tears, our childhood laughed and joined together!

Children of the earth stand tall

We made a flag using a flower cloth

In the red water that flowed on the earth

We took the colour treasure and dipped it!

 (The flowers that bloom in spring laugh

(The poet buries the mountains of corpses borne by the
flood of people)

Oh, my Eye pearls

oh, My eye pearls

Warpaths are writhing lifeless bodies

Racist inanimate bodies

You will carry them in flowing rivers!

Engage feast in the salt sea

Now you will rule the world

As one with singing one song

We shall say goodbye to a sad song

Prepare our mother for spring makeup!

(Then the sky rains. The poet sings)

We live under the sky

The mother bathes in the shower of rain pearls

Let's sing the song! Oh Birds!

Let's make stars in the soil of our eyes!

There is no boundary line in the sky

Getting there is like a lightning bolt

Lightning does not split the sky

It introduces the sky!

If the umbrella sheds the rain

Is there any way but to bathe in it?

Oh, daughter of the umbrella, weep no more

Our divine daughter will laugh and shall not cry!

(When it becomes impossible to poetry,

The world adopts this song as the world anthem.)

*****

30. In My Dream Land....

(Time before dawn
My dream is the river bank of the earth.
Under the shadow of a tiny small sura punnai tree
An aged buffalo the shadow lap, enjoys thinking of
the shadow as mud pond,
It's nothing but the buffalo's dumb dreams…

In the temple of God of Sorrow
As a resounding prayer song
It floats in from somewhere
The hymnal of the single cuckoo!

Oh! Near the ferry terminal
He is the great poet of our nation
Comrade Bharti…!)

Bharti sings:
Where are you blowing from?
The poetry of my mental house!
To decorate the life thread of spring flower

The hymn of the spring flower blowing
It is my little Quilt bird

From somewhere
Are you calling from somewhere?

The poetic fire of my mental house
Where are you blowing from?

Of my mind voice, Poetry fire
Where are you blowing from?

(The great soldier Lenin in a small hut covered with hay.
The song of the women heard in the acres of fields)

Field song
The parrot's forest exist
At the side of the village
Each multicolour parrot sleeping there
In the fruit's nest!
The full moonlight creates a flower bed
The storm persists east
The wings of parrots pursue to fly
Oh, the parrots are there
Winnowed paddy
Oh! Winnowed paddy!

(The dead buffalo is lying on the branch of
Surapunnai tree (Alexandrian laurel)
Quill plays the death hymn while seated)

Go to sleep! Go to sleep!
At the feet of the ages-old fire
With the ashes of breath
Go and fall asleep
Go and fall asleep

In the memories of this day
In this shadowy history of my pilgrimage
I will compose songs till the end!

On the same day
In this shadowy saga
I will fight till the end of my pilgrimage
Go and fall asleep
At the feet of the age-old millennium fire
With the ashes of breath
Go and fall asleep fall asleep

(Twilight Time, The Eminent Poet Bharti comes there.
In the expanse boundless of the songs, He consoled the
Quilt, Both connected with their mutual ideologies.)

Bharti:
For you, I am a poetic tree,
Shedtears like flowers from my tree.
I may be a one side love
The love dwells in the gold nest for you,
All is yours, my dear eye pearls!

Quilt:
Of My god of creation
I am sheltering and refuging
On your shoulders, lyrics
You are my springtime
I am your poetic shadow, too

(The eminent poet allows the cuckoo to sit on his shoulder
and the grove to rest. He sees Lenin there with a spade on
his shoulder.
Bharathi is with a quilt on his shoulder. Both embrace and a
tear of joy from Lenin's and Bharathi's four eyes. The river
Cauvery is the confluence of the Valka River. Bharati sings
passionately)

Bharti:
As evidence of tears
I sing this poetry!
At the feet of the crescent moon
Later in the night, I am looking for you.
The perennial river of the Soviet
Sings the songs of someone

With a melodious tune!
The snowy mountains of the country
Asking the name of someone
And melting the ice into rivers
That makes the spirit to thrills flow along…
Even after death, whoever gives birth
Into bread of the poor on this earth!
I convert all my wisdom
And breathe into songs
And sing from his hand's fold!
At the feet of the crescent moon
Later in the night, I am singing for you!

(Then the peasants come to see Lenin.
They explain to Bharti about their classless
social structure. The eminent poet Bharathi was excited by
the explanation. He sings again with endless
overwhelming)

Bharti:
Even after death, whoever gives birth
To bread for the impoverished on this earth!
Again and again, whoever
Give his birth as the bread of the poor
I sing about him
At the feet of the crescent moon

Later in the night, I am singing for him!

(From the Surapunnai tree, the cuckoo's anthem is heard.
But it's not a song sung earlier by Cuckoo on his friend,
Buffalo departed the world.
Yes then! From the field mound of the cultivators,
The cry of an unknown heard)
*****

31. The Flowers

O daughters of spring

Our mother earth will bear colourful lights!

The silences that make us sing

If only you could lend a vocal sound

A singing king

The praying lily flower

Humming honeysuckle

So many miracles would happen!

You are the wings of a dream

That's why you fall out in a short duration!

You are mute anklet bells hang in the creeper flag

You are the wind in the tree, smiles outward

You live in water as glowing fire flame!

After seeing the heaven,

You are the eyes of divine Mother Earth

You are sticking and lying down

You are the thirst pills made out of snowdrops

To fulfil the dehydration by the sun

 The dry flowers speak your life history

You mentor and make some eminent poets

You make some people traders, too.

To authorize the songs of beetles

You created the courtyard on poetries

You are the dreamland of playboy's dreamland

And signal combinations of fruits

You are the celestial footsteps,

Yet you've witnessed yourself upon the earthly realm

In the hum of bees

Your silence be existent

Oh, how beautiful you are!

The time god will knead the soil

To produce the divine begging bowl of love

Whenever there is a storm

Your palanquin made of leaves falls down

That's why you fall off

when there is a breeze

You are the citizens of time god land

When you tend to conquer the whole earth

Your so-called capital city, the spring weather

Destroys spring itself

O daughters of spring

If only you could raise your voice?!

*****

32. I think about the end of life of a man...!

After sunset

In the grey night

It manifests itself through the ages

In these minutes

I think about the limits of life

For this boat sector

I came with paddles

But I got only paper boats.

For this music hall

I came with lovely songs

But here,

There were only deaf people.

I prefer this footpath

As a good wayfarer

And I came

But it's a single-way path

With fewer human habitats.

It's all over

In this land

Nothing is left for me to love anymore

Apart from the medicine pills

What else is there?

In another dawn

My song is muted in these rose bushes.

Like I lost my childhood

You're going to miss me.

Before beating the full-length of age

The limit of life is meeting me.

My lung airbags starved to vanishisappeared

And lead to the end of life

I'm going to have a party on that day.

There shall not be any vibration in my last procession

With unbearable drum instruments

Blow the soft music with small flutes

And lay my body in a community habitat

Where the people's basic rights were denied

Near my grave,

Let it be a drain of wastewater

And a mosquito breeding channel

Poet of the less privileged

Would be handed over securely

At their crematorium

'Before the red spring came into possession

Your cuckoo is living no more

Tell them the story,

if they have not heard.

After me, when poets visit you

Please, don't shelter them at the wedding banquet

For Persian bulbul birds

Declare the news of the last minute of my life

There would be dawn tomorrow

And the crescent moon

As well for star flowers in the sky

Be comfort them when you pass

Message on my departure from this world

To all passers-by who meet you

Tell this story of mine

'At a very young age

He wrote like a sage

Even after death

Today he lives brightly- And

So no one should cry for me.

But

Wake up

No one should cry for me

Only my grave

Under the shade of Paneer flower trees

I prefer to take my long sleep

Under the shadows of Paneer trees

Those Paneer flower trees…!

*****

33. A Debate on the Bank of Mullai River Paddy Lands!

{On a Sunday evening, in the sundown times, the poet engaged in a debate within the lands by the River of Mullai. The debate restlessly continues the next day. The lands are experiencing some kind of debate. This poem could be referred to as the first expression of 'socialist dreams'.}

Before, long before,

On a day once,

During the early monsoon,

In the night rain,

In the pre-dawn moments,

Who sowed a seed in my humble soil?

Beneath the shade of this heavenly lamp,

Who stimulated me to discover under the open sky?

Witchcraft weaves its dance on the mud screen.

Brushes entwined with meticulousness.

Humble herbs from the slums,

A little eye.

The boats of saltwater streams,

Innocent growers of sweat,

They are the poets of Destiny's melodies,

Delightful singers!

Their sickles sway gently,

Resembling a dark crescent moon.

And the young women attentively join,

In the large harvest.

Who orchestrated the motivation?

Featuring the situations?

The youthful maidens of poetry,

Their skilful bangles transform

Hands into poetic jargon,

The river of tears that grants life,

Paying infinitely to the symphony,

In place of the fertile plains of humanity.

The skilful and young daughters

Knows the art of charcoal painting

Upon the face of the sun,

They gather leftovers on the streets,

In the city of love,

But it is the angels of gathering,

Is it not true?

The capitalists disfigure,

The footprints of skilled labourers,

Covering and camouflaging their sorrows!

In human prayers, they recite,

Class inequality is the devil's work!

They sprout from sealed tiger cages,

The pumpkin capitalists,

Bury the rice of the paddy

In their dark cells!

In the breeze of primal longing

The crowned capitalists tie…

The hands of siblings,

Exploiting veils of ignorance!

In the capital city of milking domicile,

A kingdom plagued by voracious hunger,

Ruled by virus-like kings,

The ignorance of white ants,

Attempting to destroy

The concealed golden history,

In the discourse of river waves,

They dissipate like foam!

In the golden age

In the spring century,

Those who adorn themselves

With the apparel of hunger!

In the vast expanse of time,

Like the wind, like water,

We shall align ourselves,

We shall stand united,

This is our pact and vow,

"Let's become the source of heat,

For the hearths of the poor,

Or else let's become the sun in the sky,

Or let's blaze within the sun."

*****

34. Oh, I am joining the Hippies too…!

You have cast aside the justice

Of valued beliefs

Into the aged breeze,

In the smog of gentle wind's dew,!

Upon the golden sandy beaches of Goa,

On a night tense with venom,

Within the desirable full moon's glow!

In the remaining world,

Still within the expansive courtyards

Of borderless paradise streets!

The melodious jingling of wine glasses,

Ah, I'm taking

On the Hippie culture as well!

The moon gave up its virgin purity

To the sun on their first night,

The custodian of the day,

It's your hero's body!

During the surge of

Time-based change,

Underneath the full moon's luminescence

At the river's bank,

At the beginning of the deepest fire,

The fly ash soil-borne

From that bundle of dust!

You offer farewell

And fled from this place,

And yet again, you return

In the vast silence of space,

An unending rehearsal of spiritual joy,

With the boon of LSD tablets,

Saliva has transformed into your wine,

On the delighted expansive beach,

Accompanied by the companionship

Of melodious dream boats…,

Ah, I'm embracing

The Hippie culture as well!

In the human haven of delight,

Upon the path of the mind's journey,

Repeatedly involved in profound love,

Altering the very soul

Of love into a stranger!

By maintaining distance from the boundaries

Of nation, language, religion, and community,

Through the touch of melodious fingertips,

Ah, I'm embracing

The Hippie culture as well!

Ah, I'm embracing the Hippie culture as well!

*****

35 The Call Girls

We are children of beautiful nights

We are minions of Cupid too!

By breaking the prison of chastity

We are being arrested!

Because the gods tasted the elixir of the Milky sea

We serve our lip's elixir to monsters!

In our court of law, discipline is punished

We sell our nirvana

For buying clothes for us!

The bed becomes an incredible

Image of the cradle by us!

We are affordable editions of the Cupid Press

Because we give birth to artificial birth to our smiles

It occurs to our tears artificial death!

Some say, in our red eyes

The saffron robes of the monks are visible!

If we were born during the time of Caesar

We don't have to offer confession to popes

And seek absolution!

Oh! Kings of justice

You are the only one who never collects tolls from us!

That's why, Still,

there No idol was erected for

Patanjali

In dietary fat, for those who are hungry

In starvation, we are the food for them!

We never knew children's hunger

Because we are the children of hunger

Even on our first night

Sweat scent sprinkled on the beds

We are slaves

That is why, in our empire,

The sun doesn't arise

 And there is no sunset!

*****

36. You have made me a SOCIALIST

Oh, my long-standing friends!

I distance myself from the illogical praise

Of your voice relationships!

Wherever the gentle breeze roams,

Carrying my flag,

They recite my verses within my heart!

Wherever the boats of those

Those who abuse workers live in less means

Sail through wild storms,

They agonize over enduring

With the paddles;

Wherever the era of youth rises

Under the shade of daytime clouds,

There, I imagine, tides flow across

The surface of waves!

Oh, my long-term friends!

Even if your paths have deviated,

You ornamented me into a Socialist!

The pleasure garden "Razor grass"

And the just seeker's blanket,

The philosophy of the space,

And expressions of sorrow,

Oh, those who have reached

Great spiritual heights!

In the temple of Mother Earth,

In the forefront

Of your place of worship,

Where labourers typically

Drop beads of sweat,

There I recite verses for the

Ground laborer's efforts!

Oh, performers of

The 'Dark Age' spirituality!

Although you might have misconstrued

Your directions,

You created me into a Socialist!

Oh, offspring of the world,

You were wetting the life roots of mankind

With the sweat of your foreheads,

Oh, my hard-working comrades!

From now on,

My poems shall burn

The insignificance of society!

All my words shall stand

As enemies against deep silences,

Oh, my hard-working comrades!

You, everyone and all,

Summon me to fight for your rights!

Now, you have grafted me as a 'Socialist'!

*****

37. The Black Flowers!

Previously,

it existed as springtime,

The initial blossoms gently fall away,

No separation in the territory of time,

The evening sky was painted over with shades,

The crescent boat sails in the clouds of the sky,

Upon our narrow little street,

A pilgrim found his way to this place.

In anticipation of the present day,

Enduring a deep darkness in a lifetime

Moonlight replacing the dark,

My dear young ladies,

The golden nest of the youthful morn,

Within the boundaries of our small street,

A pilgrim appears at this place,

What could this be?

Within the grasp of the pilgrim,

He presents his demands for a price.

Is it a soul filled with dark?

Or a dream of firewood charcoal?

Does the petal bear a black smile?

What does it signify?

Shining flower!

Shining flower!

The deep night spirit

Similar to a dream of firewood charcoal,

Wearing a dense and dark smile,

There exists the black blossom.

"Within the domain of art,

In the time of seasonal spring,

An eye opens to a black shining flower,

Intense heat infuses,

It is the slave of the golden coin,

Abstain from adorning it during the full moon.

Within the grasp of the pilgrim,

He presents his demands for a price.

"Your garden,

Within the depths of the mind's fertile soil,

Sprinkle this seed,

In the blanket thick of the darkness,

On a lonely night,

This black flower blooms;

Abstain from adorning it during the full moon!

In the limitless breadth of the sky,

Occupy in playful recreations with a feather,

Our white bird flies here

And plucks the flower and runs away,

Abstain from adorning it during the full moon!

The pilgrim who demands the price for the flower,

Strolls on his path!

In our garden,

The black flower blooms flourish abundantly,

In the meditative moments in profound darkness,

There stands the rustic shelter!

Fashioned from humble materials like leaves,

Bathes in the soft glow of the full moon,

Our narrow street comes to life by night,

Garlands with the presence of young ladies!

He recounted a fiction

Wherein a pilgrim stepped upon the moon,

Having alighted from a royal white bird!

The cuckoo weeping of death sounds,

In our enclosure;

Petals from the flowers fall away,

One by one in its time,

In every corner of the world,

The black flower blossoms,

Once again, a season,

Once again, a full moon day,

The emaciated black flower shall not bloom again;

We won't let it bloom."

The voices of ladies,

Once again

the season,

Once again, a night of full moon,

The same voice of ladies,

The same dialogue,

Once again, a season,

Once again, a night of full moon,

Grey threads upon my head,

In our narrow street,

The voices of young ladies resound,

In the soul of darkness night,

The dreams of the firewood charcoal,

The smiles of the darkest petals,

He speaks some philosophy,

In our memories,

Until the end of time,

The Shining flower shall not fade away,

In the future season may come,

Another night of a full moon,

In the ears of my grave bed,

The same dialogue continued by our young ladies,

The season comes again with a full moon night

Still the flower blooms in a shining color!

*****

38. The First Poetry

Mother Tamizh is knotted with my soul,

You foster and cultivate me!

You Blossom within me!

I familiarized you with the realm of fame,

I'm unique, not to be disremembered!

She taught me to play with words;

Words can't be enough to praise you!

Charmed me to disregard the world,

Though the poet thinks,

Claiming it's for toddy!

Moral folks shall revoke the 'prohibition act',

Seek immunity, don't fade away!

Within you, the soul of life,

To flood the world and compose a verse,

To depict difficult and awe-inspiring ponderings,

Why do you fade away so prematurely?

Whose expression can?

I behold other than my mother's?

What puzzle is this?

Burdened is my expression!

By consuming the spirit of honey from the flowery life,

I appeal to the flying bee!

Pour our tears, salty as seawater;

Don't be wooed by the appeal of poetry!

Like the rich house hen's eggs

Cracking a ploughman's grinding stone,

Approach the intoxicated

Mountain-minded poet,

Can you defeat insignificance?

Let flaming eyes awaken!

Every shoulder united,

Let daylight rise!

Through heroic verses,

Let tongues vibrate with passion,

The thirst for justice

Shall stir every daring,

Let it flourish; fanatical war chants,

The originator is gone;

Grief-stricken,

I am, Desire emerges to assault,

What recourse do I have?

The celestial sky's moon,

You remain undisrupted,

Whence did you acquire your glow?

Delighted garden, Oh honey-flower,

Arisen from the lifeless earth's flower,

Did I thrive even after?

The nectar's depletion? Why?

Why do you stay awake?

Ah! Ah! Ah! Darkness,

Where do you reside?

Oh, at liberty! Where is our ruler?

Oh! All these written drawing lines

On the floor are desolate!

The plantain tree became ripe,

Our garden;

The fierce cyclone dissolves

As other flowers elevate,

Witness the cruelty

Of bending before the storm,

Rapidly, bottle with a protective shield,

Within our humble frames,

Only cries endure,

We abandoned the leaves' shedding fire,

We floated down the two-eyed river!

Like us, amidst the tempestuous sea,

Who is the mad one?

In the heavenly abode,

We resemble you,

The moon that lingers like tea,

Who rubbed the gold?

The Beautiful,

Blissful women are born to weep!

Who created this affliction?

Upon the earth?

Reddish tears, declare this,

Who is the architect of all?

Who is the Creator?

Flowers! You have vanished

Without blooming!

Earthquakes! Depart! Vanish,

You who cause a blaze! Oh vast sea,

You are buried within this earth,

Oh, full moon in the sky,

You pursue the pattern of your routine!

You distressed us with your mourning!

*****

39. The Story of Subtraction

The account owed to me

Borrows from a neighbour!

And subtracts the numbers for me,

My friends are my credits,

And I am the expenses.

Life flies high with its wings as we spend without hesitancy.

The plus is a burden for all;

It reminds the story of the crucifixion.

Multiplication is a symbol of resistance,

And division is a symbol of our heirs,

I am the symbol of life,

The adjudicatory forum of accounts!

Addition and multiplication

Create garbage in the streets!

Dumping, overflowing,

It is visible everywhere along the streets!

Collecting sugarcane for festivals

Multiplies the celebrations of weddings too,

And brings a way for happiness!

Though, subtracting old rubbish garbage

From living spots makes the festival

More of a reality!

Functions like indication

Of ensuring safety or disposal

Of old things reflect the self-immolation

Of garbage only!

No matter how it comes

And whatever happens in life's layout,

Even if things multiply and are deductible of waste,

Only after the subtraction of all,

Until the end,

Brings a way of life that brings peace!

In the discourse of life,

Multiply the efforts to add prosperity!

And subtract the sorrows.

My identity symbol, 'minus,' is so tiny,

Even if it is a small line,

I am the symbol of wisdom depictions!

In modern painting,

The picture itself denotes like small lines.

Here, I confine the paintings

Within the lines!

I am the thought process;

I always bring a small shell

That contains a pearl.

If there is no subtraction,

The epics of the world do not exist!

If there is no such character like King George!

The birth of the Russian Nation is not possible

On the world map!

If there is no character like Macbeth,

The drama of Shakespeare is not included

In the literature!

Oh, my dear friends,

You are the questions;

Hence, I am the answer!

I am the donor; you are the receiver!

A man who adds customary literature,

That is the prime duty of disciples!

Subtraction exists everywhere.

If the tradition subtracts something,

That will turn into modern technology.

If you subtract leaves from sugarcane,

That poses the sweetest cane!

If you subtract impurity in public services,

That turns honest services to society!

If you divide good plans into parts,

That fine-tunes the public welfare policies.

If you divide policy into actions,

That enhances the prosperity of the public!

The rulers aim at new income for the state,

But that never makes people happy.

And if the rulers subtract the new taxes,

That brings more delight to the citizens

And enhances social justice among the states!

Man subtracts carbon dioxide

From fossil fuel in motor vehicles

To accelerate his journey!

While cobras shed their old skins,

Chameleons change their colors,

All indicating the existence

Of dangers around man!

If other symbols become rose gardens

On the surface of mountains!

The symbol of subtraction

Lives like the lily flower

At the bottom of the hills!

To appear beautiful,

She subtracts her excess flush

From her body when looking at someone!

The perennial rivers

And the vast ocean exist

As they subtract raindrops.

The symbols in math resemble flowers

On the plain land,

But the subtraction symbol is like a deer

In that plain land!

Their symbol does not get subtracted

From anywhere but moves here and there only!

During the concert of the cuckoo,

Subtraction is the noise of the dove's wings!

The symbol minus exhibits

Its specialty on many occasions!

If you subtract the Nile River,

Egypt cracks into a desert!

If you subtract the full moon at night,

Darkness starves for full moonlight!

The autumn period is the subtraction;

The spring climate was born after that!

History subtracts the Warfield

And hoists the flag of peace!

All children leave their mother worm

After subtracting their mature time!

When you subtract your natural age,

You turn youthful in attributes!

Subtraction is the symbol of life

That transforms barren land into fertile land!

After exercising the subtraction process,

if you subtract the east, you shall get daylight!

The sun rises in the morning

In the beauty of subtracting

The previous evening!

 I search for the answers

In the narrow streets of the city,

Though subtracted during the day

And housed after sunlight!

I am the center for education,

A person like a buried grape garden,

And the waterfall hidden,

Artificially in a cage!

I am the closed garden

In Taj Mahal grounds!

Dear friends, you are the food,

But I am the hunger!

The subtraction in a smile is sorrow,

And the subtraction of dresses at night, yes,

That is your first night!

If you grow unwanted bushes along

The Forest Jasmine in your fence line,

I subtract them as a gardener.

I subtract the skins of bamboo

To get the flute to blow sweet music!

Subtract stones embedded

More than the mountain

To create a beautiful statue!

I subtract shells to obtain pearls!

When the cuckoo sings,

I subtract my words

To enjoy the sweet melodies of the bird!

I subtract the bullock cart

To bring a train on rails!

When a beautiful woman subtracts her virginity,

She attains motherhood!

I subtracted the writing pen

From my study room,

To bring the printing machine!

I subtracted religion from my heart,

And I found humanity there!

Many times, flowers are subtracted

From the garden by mistake,

And the leaves in the plant flourish!

Subtracting pimples and beard

From the face of a man,

That is my foreword.

I subtract capitalism from society;

That is my inference!

*****

40. Fire Wood

The rising sun burns through the night.

I will throw the burning sun as firewood.

For the benefit of the poor, to cook their food.

I will speak to the dark in the language of light

*****

41. Slavery!

When our nation decolonized,

I felt enslaved,

That is the day

I was admitted to primary school!

*****

42. Flower in Rough Cradle

The rough cloth in the cradle,

But the baby's skin is as soft as a flower!

Who is this?

You are the treasure

of the mother's womb!

 You exercise your kicks

When I hug you,

Synonymous with my warmth!

Your spitting turns

Into my tender coconut water!

*****

43. The Beauty

The beauty of a lovely woman

Resides in her eyes!

White dots glorify the beauty

Of a leaping deer!

The beauty of the reddish rays

Dabbles in its burning fire!

The beauty of Mother Nature's spring

Admires in the presence

Of her fish children!

The beauty of the conch lies

In its whitish color shades!

The beauty of the chest lodges

In the sandalwood paste!

The beauty of a woman's neck

Adores in the golden necklace!

My kid brother's beauty speaks

In a sweet childish voice!

*****

Epilogue

The voices within "Black Flowers" resonate powerfully, serving as a emotional reminder of the vibrant need to amplify marginalized voices and advocate for equality and justice for all. They offer a message of empowerment and resilience to anyone grappling with the burdens of societal expectations and discrimination. Reading more than one poem per day may not be feasible, as each poem is more than just a collection of words; it's an immersive experience that deserves time and reflection. It's understandable why Dr.Sanna Ratnavel prefers the powerful words as chosen by Eminent Poet.Na.Ka. Indeed, it is a difficult task.-**M.S.Dhandapany, Senior Journalist.**

"The Black Flowers" -Through its evocative imagery and heartfelt language, the poem becomes a beacon of hope for those navigating dark and difficult times. By highlighting the strength and courage of marginalized voices, it inspires empathy and solidarity, fostering a sense of connection and understanding across diverse experiences of oppression. Every one should read these verses to understand 'what is a poem?'My friend Dr Sanna Ratnavel is a powerful writer as Kaviyarasu Na.Ka in reality-**Er.J.Suresh, Professional Engineer (Senior).**

"Voices of the Third Gender" resonates deeply with any marginalized or oppressed community, capturing the universal experience of struggling against societal norms and discrimination. The poem's themes of resilience and empowerment extend beyond the third gender community, offering solace and validation to anyone facing adversity or oppression. -**T.Krishnamoorthy, B.Sc., (Agri), Natural Farming & Agro Consultant.**

The Eminent Poet **Na. Kamarasan** has expressed that his primary motivation for writing poetry and lyrics has never been fame or fortune, but rather a desire to elevate Tamizh literature to a global standard.

*****

www.ingramcontent.com/pod-product-compliance
Lightning Source LLC
Chambersburg PA
CBHW021449150726
47989CB00001B/456